"Bill Huebsch has a special gift for naming the foibles of mis-education in spirituality that most of us have been subjected to. He targets our misconceptions about prayer as a formal activity addressed to a distant God, an activity in which we feel woefully inadequate until we realize that that is not what prayer is about at all.

"Through the graceful use of biblical images, Huebsch leads us from the distant unpredictable God of institutions to Jesus' reliable Abba. Through his descriptions of everyday life and his straightforward exposure of its empty materialism and its unmet spiritual needs, he leads us to discover the presence of God in our own experience; this more than anything else will lead to the renewal of spiritual life for which so many long."

Carolyn Osiek, R.S.C.J.
Professor of New Testament
Catholic Theological Union

"Huebsch does a masterful job of presenting a practical piety for Christians involved in the affairs of contemporary society. He does so in an easy poetic style that adds richness and depth to the spiritual vision he presents. Especially attractive about the approach is its solid grounding in present-day biblical scholarship. Huebsch's biblical piety leads readers to deep involvement in the world around them, not into serene escapism. With this volume Huebsch clearly enhances his reputation as one of America's most creative exponents of emerging lay spirituality."

John T. Pawlikowski, O.S.M., Ph.D.
Professor of Social Ethics
Catholic Theological Union
Senior Editor, *New Theology Review*

a New Look at Prayer

Searching for Bliss

Bill Huebsch

TWENTY-THIRD PUBLICATIONS
Mystic, Connecticut

Other books by Bill Huebsch:

A Spirituality of Wholeness: The New Look at Grace
Rethinking Sacraments: Holy Moments in Daily Living

Available from Twenty-Third Publications

Third printing 1992

Twenty-Third Publications
185 Willow Street
P.O. Box 180
Mystic, CT 06355
(203) 536-2611
800-321-0411

ISBN 0-89622-458-9
Library of Congress Catalog Card No. 90-71136

Contents

~~

a NEW LOOK at PRAYER

Introduction

In 1966 I was a sophomore in high school at Crosier Seminary in Onamia, Minnesota, a boarding school for college prep students. That fall I was part of a fantastic intramural touch football team. We won almost all our games, which seemed miraculous to me, a non-athlete. What I wanted more than anything was for us to win the final tournament. I'd never won a single athletic trophy in my life, and this seemed to be my moment.

On the morning of the big game, I decided to go down to the small chapel in the seminary and ask God for victory. I wasn't exactly sure God behaved in this way. I wasn't sure God intervened directly in high school football games, but I really wanted to win and I thought I'd hedge my bets and cover all my bases. Anyway, what could it hurt?

So I headed down to pray. But as I pushed open the door of the chapel, I was horrified to find that the entire opposing team was already there! They beat me to it! They had asked first, and besides, I was all alone and they were all there; I could see there was no hope!

For many people, prayer is a consumer commodity. We pray for things: rain, peace, health, success. And when we get what we ask for, we believe our prayer is responsible for it. If we don't get it, we switch into another way of thinking and wonder whether we prayed wrong, or whether God just knew better, or whether someone else deserved to win this one more than we did.

We think of prayer as something we do in order to get something else. It's a commodity to be traded for favors from God, who, in our judgment, would not bestow these favors without sufficient supplication.

This popular view of prayer is in tension with "prayer" as presented in scripture. What we learn when we listen to the gospels and the early mothers and fathers of the church is that prayer is indeed "receiving," but what is received is the energy and love of God in the life of the one who prays. Prayer is not a business transaction with God. It's the natural inclination of humans to be wrapped up in the power of the Force of Life, the Creator, the Artist in the garden who made us all.

Our role is simply to pause and allow prayer to emerge in us, naturally. It is for us to turn down the volume of our own words long enough to hear the Word of God. It is for us to listen. To *listen*. God is speaking if we would only listen.

But how does God actually speak to us in prayer? Karl Rahner has asked this question poignantly in his book *Christians at the Crossroads*. There he begins to form a partial answer for us. In this book I will take up his suggestions, along with those of Thomas Merton, Abraham Heschel, Matthew Fox, St. John of the Cross, the Desert Contemplatives, the Mystics, Henri Nouwen, and some of the great Zen Masters. This book explores the mystery of prayer, the grace of presence, and the listening to which prayer invites us.

For Whom Do I Write This?

Parents who want to teach their children to know God will find in these reflections on prayer a source of strength. Helping children trust their inner voices, their inborn divine wisdom, is a great parental calling.

Adult Christians who wonder whether God still speaks in our day and in their lives can search for an answer in this book. God not only speaks, but is, in a sense, never silent. God's energy, power, and voice never leave us.

Jews who wish to draw nearer to Yahweh will see in this book a path to the Mountain of God. We Christians and Jews share such a rich, profound, divine journey. We traveled from Ur together with Abraham and Sarah. We were slaves together in Egypt. We crossed the barren desert together with Moses and Miriam. We danced together before the Ark. We sinned together in the face of prophecy. We have waited together, waited for the day when the lion and lamb will play together, and we are still waiting for that day. As we wait we can share another journey together, this one: a journey to the heart of God.

Catechists and teachers might use this book as a guide to teach about prayer. Their students, whether children or adults or catechumens, will grow more able to hear the voice of God.

Preachers and homilists who struggle to know how to speak about God's voice in the din of our culture can find courage here to more boldly proclaim that God is speaking and that we can hear only when we confidently stand before the powers of the outer voices of our day and age.

Pastoral care workers, visitors to the sick and imprisoned, ministers to persons with AIDS, all who struggle to hear God's voice in the midst of their pain will find in these words a way to approach God once and for all, sometimes for the last time before their death.

Those whom the church does not legitimate but who

have learned to trust the voice of God in their lives—
women seeking full ministry, persons living in broken commitments, gays and lesbians (including those living together in permanent union), couples who struggle with family
planning, even those who have stopped praying, stopped
attending Mass, and stopped listening to God—this book is
also for them. No official of a church can stop God from
speaking in the ordinary lives of people, no matter who the
people are. No one can draw lines about who's in and who's
out, or exclude anyone from hearing the voice of God.

Newcomers to the church, especially those making a journey of faith through the catechumenate, will find here that
God is already speaking in their lives, that God is calling
them in their inner selves, their depths. They will learn to
dance with God, touching grace.

Small communities who seek to discern God's voice
among their members might share this book together, chapter by chapter. The excitement we all feel when we share
life in small communities is increased exponentially when
we also share what we hear God saying in our lives and
through our times.

The Format

I've chosen not to present these reflections in common paragraph format because the ideas here lend themselves more
readily to a sense-line style. Reflecting on God's voice, like
following it, resists being boxed. Sense lines allow me to
juxtapose ideas, compare thoughts, isolate key words or
phrases. They also allow readers the space they need for
imaginations to rest; they offer space for the right brain to
create its own text.

The Title

The Second Vatican Council's document "The Church in the
Modern World" provides the starting point for our thinking

on prayer here (paragraph 16): "Conscience is the most secret core and sanctuary of man *(sic)*. There he is alone with God, *whose voice echoes in his depths*" (italics added).

Listening to that voice of God in our depths leads us to an inner life of joy and peace that could only be called "blissful." That bliss, on which Joseph Campbell has also written, is certainly the goal of the Christian life since Jesus himself assured us that he had come "to make our joy complete," to lead us to bliss. Living a prayerful life and living a blissful one are closely linked. One doesn't seem possible without the other. The bliss we seek waits within us to be drawn forth so that we may live in joy!

Karl Rahner may have said this best: "The theological problem today is the art of drawing religion out of a person, not pumping it in. The art is to help people become what they really are...."

That is the goal and purpose of this book.

Acknowledgments

I am learning to trust the voice of God myself every day. I write about it better than I practice it. But my family, my friends, my co-workers, my teachers—all are helping me learn more and more about this.

Rev. Tony Kill, of Park Avenue Congregational Church in Arlington, Massachusetts, has shared his sermons with me, and I have accordingly shared his thoughts here with you. David Belt, a young priest of the Archdiocese of Omaha, led me with his insights to the living water with Jesus and the woman at the well in John's gospel. Dirk and Clara Nohre from Milwaukee, Wisconsin, provide a constant cadence in my life, reminding me gently but firmly of God's continual voice. Morrie Hartman, a companion on the journey, has provided me a regular place to clarify God's voice, to sort truth from falsehood. Ramona and Russ Kadow, sister and brother to me, have challenged me, stretched me, opened my ears to hear. Finally, Dan Conlin, friend and colleague in the vineyard, has provided me a model for contemplative listening prayer which I still seek to emulate. He has re-introduced to me a little monk who lives within a corner of my life.

There are many others, of course, but these eight women and men have generously contributed to this project.

Conclusion

Let me take you back with me to that small chapel at Crosier Seminary in the fall of 1966. I did finally go into the chapel that morning, still intending to ask God for victory. I knelt down, realizing I was in the heart of the enemy, aware that I was the only one from the other team who was present. The senior captain was leading a prayer.

But he wasn't praying for victory! He was praying for charity, for fairness, and for an honest game. He asked God for the inner strength to be a humble winner—or a graceful loser—and he prayed that, in the final analysis, our lives together in our community would be made more joyful, that our brotherhood would grow stronger from this contest on the playing field.

He took the wind out of my sails!

I learned something that day that I've never forgotten. God is love, and the one who lives in love, lives in God and God lives in him or her. God's power affects our inner lives, our hearts, and *we* affect the world. God's intervention, if we can call it that, is an intervention of love in our inner lives. We need but open our minds and hearts to it.

1

~~

Learning to Hear

Most of what I learned about prayer
    as a child
    was, on the face of it,
        flatly heretical.
I'm sure my parents and teachers
    didn't mean it to be so
    because what they taught me
        is what everyone learned
        for the most part.
Their intention, I'm sure
    was a noble one:
    to help me get into a habit
    of prayer.
And since we were Americans
    we did it the old-fashioned,
        American way:
        we worked hard at it.

We were taught
about prayer
as mostly a human activity,
something we do,
and something it's a sin
not to do.
"Missing our morning prayers,"
was a venial sin
for us.
It used to appear regularly
on the old laundry lists
for confession,
somewhere between impure thoughts
and fighting with siblings.

But what we meant
was that we hadn't
"said our prayers."
The fault was all on our part
for not having done anything,
for not having worked hard enough
to pray.
The "saying" was our job,
we were supposed to do the work.
It shouldn't surprise us, then,
that we developed over time
the notion that God
was sitting in heaven
waiting to hear from us.
Our picture was of someone
sort of like Aunt Emma,
waiting for the thank-you note
after Christmas.
Poor Aunt Emma,
all alone,

going to her mailbox every day
but never getting a letter,
    like it was my job
    to keep Aunt Emma happy.
We thought about God that same way
    much of the time, didn't we?

Under this notion,
    God was the recipient of prayer
    in the same way, say,
        that a visiting bishop
        received our adulation
        as we kissed his ring.
God didn't have to do much
    in this plan.
    We did.
And our failure to work hard
    at praying,
        was what made prayer a failure.
I scarcely know a soul
    who feels that he or she prays
    often enough or well enough.
As a result,
    most people feel guilty
    about their prayer lives,
        as though they haven't done
        what they were told to do
        years ago in grade school.
And there's been so much talk
    about "how to pray"
    in recent years,
        that we have a new twist
        on this guilt today.
Now people can also feel guilty

about not having learned
the new methods of prayer.
Just the other day
someone said to me
with a perfectly straight face:
"I haven't learned how
to do Centering Prayer yet.
I realize I should,
but I just haven't had time!"
Double guilt!
What a great idea!
Not only are they not praying,
but they're not praying
the right kind of prayer!
I once knew a saintly old priest
who prayed the Divine Office
by working very hard at it.
Sometime about 11:00 PM,
after a long day of ministry,
he'd sit down
to begin "saying" the Office
and he'd start with morning prayer
for the day just ending!
Then he'd move on to the rest,
finishing finally about midnight
just making the deadline!
He prayed maybe a dozen psalms,
countless scripture readings,
refrains,
and antiphons:
but he got it all done
on time,
and that's what mattered.
But then,
and here's the amazing part,

if he happened to get done early,
he'd get himself some ice cream,
watch the late show
and wait for midnight.
Then he'd start on the next day's prayers,
beginning with morning prayer
for the day that started
after midnight!
Then he'd move on and sometimes
get all the way through Compline
of that day,
all in an effort
to be sure he got it done,
to be sure he worked at it.
By doing this,
he met every demand of the law
about prayer.
He did everything
according to the minimal obligation
based on church teaching.
But was it really prayer?

I knew this priest well,
by the way,
and knew that he also punctuated his day
with pauses for prayer,
not the official prayer,
but something very meaningful.
This form of prayer,
in which he'd simply pause
to feel God's presence before his next appointment,
or to wonder at beauty,
or to recall someone in need,
this was his "real" prayer,
and he never knew it.

Like most of us,
    he was taught to "work" at his prayer,
    just as my parents and teachers taught me.
In fact,
    the Baltimore Catechism
    gave such a definition
      of prayer as "work"
    that we thought there was no doubt.
"Prayer," the catechism said,
    "is the raising of the mind and heart
      to God."
"It is the high privilege,"
    it also said,
    "of angels and men [sic]
      to speak with God in prayer."
I think this might be
    an outright theological error
    on the face of it.

There is a heresy of faith
    called Pelagianism
    which suggests that the work of salvation
    is done by us,
      rather than by God.
Pelagius might have endorsed
    these Baltimore Catechism
    definitions of prayer;
    he might have believed
      that prayer is our job alone.
This heresy has been badly overrated
    by church leaders
    because Pelagius also had some
    very helpful insights into the faith.
Nonetheless, on this point,

our own experience seems to differ
from his theories.
It is the experience of so many of us
that there is a Force of Life
which is beyond us
and which summons us
from within.
There seems to be planted within us,
a natural orientation to God,
a basic sense of being drawn
to the artist
who made us.
We seem drawn toward God
whether we like it or not.
There is a natural urge
for us to be in communion
with our maker,
much like a child turns
to its mother and father.
This urge expresses itself in many ways,
but most of the time
it's simply a deep sense of Presence,
God with us: Emmanuel!

Let me note:
we do possess the freedom
to resist that urge within us.
We may always deny it,
hide from it
or refuse to allow it
to touch us.
But the urge remains
nonetheless.
It's an urge to communicate with God,
to hear God speak to us.

Understanding this basic inner urge
to be with God,
we could hardly say
that prayer is all on our part.
In fact, we would likely conclude
that most of prayer
is *not* on our part.
So, to contradict the words
of the Baltimore Catechism,
prayer is not a solely human effort
to raise our minds and hearts
to God.

But the catechism
did have an important insight.
We do need to be ready
for prayer.
We need to be ready
to hear the voice of God,
ready to listen,
to quiet the turmoil
within our anxious hearts
long enough to really *hear*.
So, in a sense,
we do begin in prayer
by opening our minds and hearts
to God.
Prayer remains a distant thing
for most people.
It remains a far-off goal,
something they know they should get to
when they have time
or when they can organize their lives
more fittingly.

It remains something
 people generally feel should be left
  to religious people.
A friend recently confided in me
 that she hopes
 that there are still nuns in cloisters,
 praying for the world
  because she herself
  found it so difficult to do so.
"I haven't said my prayers in a long time,"
 she told me.
  "I think *someone* should be praying."

But if there is within us
 a natural orientation to God,
 to the Creator,
 to the artist that made us,
  then wouldn't prayer also
  be natural?
Should we look outside ourselves
 for a way to hear the voice of God,
 or should we look
  into our inner journeys,
  inner pathways through life?
Shouldn't prayer be integral to life?

Let's stay with this question
 for another moment.
If indeed God is creator,
 the one who made us,
 then wouldn't it be true
  that God is still with us?
And if God is with us,

as the Hebrew Scriptures show,
as Christ clearly reveals,
and as our faith continues to unfold,
   if God is with us
   then where should we look
      for God?
Wouldn't it be true
   that becoming aware of ourselves
   is becoming aware of God?
Wouldn't discovering ourselves
   also be a discovery of God,
   if it's our real, created self
      we find?

Abraham Heschel,
   a great Jewish theologian,
   has called prayer
      an "ontological necessity,"
      which is to say,
      an "inborn hunger for God."
He echoes the teachings of Christ
   in so doing,
   and he leads us home
      with these words.
If that is true,
   if there is such an inborn hunger,
   then can prayer really
      be far away from us?

Often when we pray
   we are victims of an historical idea
   that we must summon God
   as though God were not already with us.

"Come, Holy Spirit!" we pray.
Christ did pray
    to his heavenly parent,
    but in the next breath
    he announced that heaven,
        the reign of God,
        is within us.
"Our Father in heaven,"
    becomes,
    in view of the total gospel,
    "Our Father whose reign is near,
        our Mother within...."
We hang on, though,
    to the notion that heaven
    is somehow distant,
        not the reign within.
This confusion
    is the result of all those centuries
    in which the church changed very little
    from a medieval preoccupation
        with the dark side of the world.
We built buildings
    that would point us toward God.
    Their spires reached to heaven,
    away from us,
        away from earth,
        away from the mundane,
        away from everyday life.
In so doing,
    were they also reaching
    away from the Incarnation?
We folded our hands the same way,
    neatly pointed toward heaven,
        "up there."
All these centuries later we still

look for God in buildings.
We still point our hands and hearts
    upward and outward.

But in fact,
    prayer is not a leaving of ourselves
    to go to God,
        is not a movement away from earth.
It is instead a radical
    movement to the center of life,
    to the center of creation.
It is a finding of God
    in the present,
    in the world,
    in our lives.
Prayer leads us to our very center.

Jesus, we must remember,
    was tempted in the desert
    to abandon his mission
        which was to be human.
"Turn these stones into bread"
    he was tempted,
    something no human could do.
But he resisted
    because he knew that being fully
    and authentically human
        is to be near to God.
The message of the Incarnation
    is that we are *not* called to be God.
The story of the Garden
    helps us to see this.
Adam and Eve were teased

into believing that they could be
like God.
They fell for the trap
and we have fallen for it, too.
The message of the Incarnation
is that we are to be fully human,
joyfully alive as people,
not grasping to be like God.

In prayer
we gather together,
all the fragments of our lives,
and we find in them
the hand of God,
molding us as a potter.
In prayer
we take what is divided,
ruptured,
scattered in our lives
and give it to God
who folds it all together
to form beautiful vessels.

In prayer
we hear the voice of God
when we hear our own "word,"
which is expressed in love,
and is created and ordered toward God.

Reflect

What is the story of your attempt to learn to
pray? What supports you most in your desire to pray? What distracts you?

2

~~

God's Way of Speaking

This chapter takes up a question
   that is at the very heart
   of our prayer.
It's a question we fear to ask
   because we know its difficulties
   and we don't want them.
Over time,
   each of us has developed
   a notion of who God is.
Each of us has prayed
   or not prayed
   to that God
      with this or that form of prayer
      and with this or that result.
We've grown comfortable
   with these understandings.

They're safe
  and they keep God out of our daily lives.
When we enter the process of
  questioning
  and challenging,
    we will also upset
    and challenge ourselves.
But we must ask anyway:
  Who is this God
    to whom we pray ?
What kind of things
  can this God do for us,
  can this God do *to* us?
Where does this God live,
  what realms does God inhabit?
And who does this God favor?
  Does God favor us?
  Or does God favor our enemies?
How do we even begin to ask about this,
  how do we inquire into God
  who is wholly Other,
  absolutely Transcendent,
  the great Mystery?
How do we ask the questions?
  How do we form the answers?

Yet asking and answering,
  at least for our times
  and for us,
    can greatly enhance our prayer.
Asking and answering the question
  of who God is
  can lead us to inner harmony
  and to more wonderful living.

There is no doctrine about God
    locked into place
    for all time,
    in the church or outside of it.
There is no final word on this,
    nothing definite that isn't soft,
    no certainty we can't question.
Revelation is in God's hands,
    after all,
    not ours.
And apparently, revelation continues to occur.

Let's begin by looking back
    at some of the notions of God
    that have helped form our own.
The deities of ancient peoples
    seemed a curious bunch.
The gods of Greek and Roman mythology,
    the gods of the Norse,
    those of other native peoples
    and the ancient Hebrew gods
    were often moody,
        capricious,
        and arbitrary.
They took sides in war
    and made trouble in times of peace.
They could be begged,
    bargained with,
    and cajoled.
Having them on your side
    meant prosperity,
    fair weather,
    good sailing,
    and safety.

But having the gods against you
　　could spell disaster!
Like the sailor who fell from grace
　　with the sea,
　　　　falling from grace with one of these gods
　　　　　　meant danger.
They were quick to punish
　　those they did not like,
　　quick to retaliate,
　　quick to seek revenge.
They were, indeed,
　　not to be toyed with.

The gods of these people
　　were thought to live in dwellings
　　beyond the earth.
Some apparently inhabited
　　a sort of underworld
　　while others lived on Mount Olympus
　　or some other distant,
　　　　unapproachable place.
They did not,
　　in any case,
　　live on earth.
They were not part of the human family,
　　not Emmanuel, not "God with us."
　　But they were fully capable, it seems,
　　　　of human moods and caprice.

These were demanding gods,
　　certain of their wants for people
　　and willing to punish those
　　　　who disobeyed.

One of the gods of the Aztec people,
  for example,
  demanded repeated human sacrifice
    in order to be satisfied.
Others required payments of food,
  animal sacrifices,
    virgins cast into volcanoes,
  and the like.
One famous god
  demanded the bloody sacrifice
  of his own son
    in order to be appeased.

Is this how our God speaks to us?
  making demands and judgments?
  dealing with us arbitrarily?
  condemning some of us to death
    and calling others to life?
Does this describe
  the God of Jesus,
  the *Abba* he revealed to us?
It seems not,
  but, oddly,
  many Christians retain
  an image of a god
  that varies little
    from the notion just described.
Christians have an image of God
  as an individual person
  with a psychological profile
  that differs very little
    from their own.
The god imagined by many believers
  is moody and arbitrary,

and can be begged,
and who even *wants* to be begged.
This is a god who sometimes answers prayer
but often does not,
presumably because this god knows
better than we
our own needs.
At other times this imagined god
does not answer prayer
because the pray-er doesn't deserve it,
or because the pray-er didn't pray
hard enough
or long enough
or with the right words.
As young Christians,
growing in understanding
and coming to terms with God,
we were often taught about a god
who strongly disliked those
who fought with siblings,
missed prayer times,
told lies,
touched themselves sexually,
or allowed impure thoughts to linger.
We were taught about a god
who would "get us"
if we didn't watch out.
This is the ancient image of god.
Parents are often supported
in teaching this notion of god
to their children
by the church.
Church teachers sometimes use this notion of God
to justify and explain
everything from stillbirth
to plane crashes.

"God wanted to take that child home to heaven"
or "God needed that child
more than we do."

Beyond that,
    this god whom children are meeting
    is one who wants everyone
        to go to Mass on Sunday,
        to receive the sacraments,
        and to meet the fiscal needs
        of the church.
God and God's rules
    take on new dimensions
    and are presented with even more certainty
    as the young person grows into puberty.
Now this god is concerned about sex
    more than anything else,
    and enforcing rules about sexuality
    is a preoccupation with this god.
God is "used" to enforce a moral code
    and "divine law" is summoned
    to drive home the points of it.
Some parents and teachers resort to this
    when they teach young people
        that hearing the laws of the church
            is equivalent to hearing God's voice.
This imagined god is one
    who sends rain if we ask properly,
    one who protects us on auto trips,
    one who takes certain lives
        and leaves others
        according to some divine plan
        unknown to us.
This is a god
    who can be appeased by sacrifice,

who loves to be praised,
and who continues to fight
a great cosmic battle
against Lucifer.
This is a god who is male,
lives in heaven,
and is addressed through one-way prayer.
Growing up with this notion,
and having it reinforced in church circles
over and over again,
it's no wonder few Christians have had
an *Abba* experience
like Jesus had.
The God we have just described
is not the God of Jesus.
The primary goal
of Jesus' life and ministry
is to introduce us to his *Abba*,
his creative parent,
his source and destiny.
Jesus' whole life,
his whole journey and purpose
seems to be wrapped up in this:
that those who know him
would know *Abba*.
Jesus' relationship with God
was intimate and familiar
and this distinguished him
from other prophets of his day.
Abba is an Aramaic word,
Aramaic being the language
that Jesus spoke most of the time.
Abba is one of the words
we are most sure that Jesus himself
must have used.

He referred to God this way
   at crucial moments
   in the gospel stories.
In the earliest manuscripts
   of the gospel of Mark,
   this word appears in this Aramaic form.
The word carried such a profound sense
   of relationship to God
   that it could not even be translated
   into Greek or Latin!
But it lodged itself
   in the collective memory of the community
   who most likely used it
      as Jesus did.
It suggests a union with God
   which was very close,
   even inseparable.
His relationship with God as *Abba*
   seems to have been Jesus' source
   of life and identity
   and *Abba* was also Jesus' destiny.
Jesus certainly is not the only one
   who used this word
   but his use appears to be unique
      in its meaning
      intensity
      and purpose.
The word itself suggests an intimacy
   that we can't really define.
We are at a loss
   to explain
   how close Jesus and *Abba* really were.

God, for Jesus,
   was not some distant reality,

acting separately from human life.
No, God, for Jesus, was personal,
    not an object outside him
    but the inner life,
        that graced
        and permeated him.
When Jesus thought about himself,
    he also thought about God.
When Jesus revealed himself,
    he also revealed God.

So it is with us as well.

When we talk about God
    we are really also talking
    about ourselves.
And when we talk about ourselves,
    we are really also talking about God.
God is not outside the world,
    outside us,
    outside our souls.
God's life is within us:
    "...the reign of God is within."

The descriptions of the gods
    of ancient peoples
    that we considered earlier
        were really descriptions
        of the ancient peoples themselves.

And our inner notion of who God is,
    the one we carry around within us,
    is also a description of us.

Jesus' *Abba* was not like other gods,
    not like the gods of the ancients,
    not a distant being,
        not a moody judge,
        not an absent ruler.
Jesus' *Abba* was near,
    always at his side,
    the source of love,
        the truth,
        the destiny of his life.
Abba is a mystery,
    of that there is little question.
    But the mystery is one of depth,
        not of confusion.
The mystery of *Abba* is like the depth of love,
    the brilliance of light,
    the profundity of truth.
It is not that we cannot understand
    but that there is so much to know,
    so much revealed,
        constantly,
        daily,
        and so near to us
            that we can never plumb it all.
In a sense,
    Abba is so near,
    so much an integral part of being human
    that we cannot escape God's love.
There is nowhere to hide,
    as the Scriptures tell us,
    nowhere we could not be found.
There are no moods in Jesus' *Abba*,
    none at all.
God is sure,
    steady,

relentless in loving us.
The power of Jesus' *Abba*
  is not used to overpower others,
  or to "lord it over them...."
It's the power of commitment,
  solidarity,
  forgiveness,
  and peace.
It's a power that transforms
  but it does so from within our souls,
  within our communities.
This powerful, loving experience of God,
  this *Abba* experience,
  is one that even sinners
    have available to them.
There is no revenge in the God of Jesus,
  no retaliation,
  no desire for repayment.

In short,
  Jesus illumines for us his *Abba*,
  his source and his destiny.
We ourselves now find
  that this illumination continues
    in Christ,
    the risen One.
We find illumined in our lives
  a depth of mystery,
  a power of love,
  a revelation of truth,
  a movement toward wholeness,
    oneness,
    holiness.
We are in communion with God,

intimate,
deep communion.
And this communion,
this intense moment of God's presence,
this experience of *Abba*
is prayer.

God's way of speaking
as revealed by Jesus
is gentle, yet firmly loving.
It is near at hand,
so that we must listen closely
to our own hearts to hear it.
God speaks in this prayer,
not with words as such,
and certainly not the kind of words we utter
when we speak with one another.
The "dialogue" with God,
as Karl Rahner has described it
consists in God speaking all right,
but not with many words.
In prayer, Rahner says,
God speaks a single word:
the life of the one who prays.
It is our life that God speaks,
a life oriented toward mystery
and open to the expanding horizon
of God's energy and love.
We have been taught
that we should expect to hear
God speaking rules and regulations,
dos and don'ts,
systems of morality and behavior;
judgments,

inquisitions,
investigations,
condemnations,
and excommunications.
We've expected revelation to consist
in a plan for our lives,
a list of the things we are "supposed"
to be doing.
We've looked for God's voice
in a sky opening
and a great voice finally telling us
what's what.

But that is not how God speaks,.
not ordinarily anyway.
God's voice is a whisper,
which we, like Elijah,
must bend our ears to hear.
It is the fragile voice of a young man,
scarcely able to understand
his own fate,
following his destiny to a Cross.
That young man's moment of truth
with his *Abba*,
reveals an alluring
yet frightening closeness.

So, we are what is spoken by God.
Prayer is listening to this word,
listening carefully,
discerning God's voice
in the din of voices
that surround us.

God is always creating us,
 always pouring Spirit and Word
 into us.
The place where God meets us
 is the privileged place
 of the Self,
  a place created by God
  for just such a meeting.
Here we open that Self in freedom
 and hear the grand utterance
 of our own name!
Here we are shaped and formed,
  here we are made whole and holy,
  here we are able to know *Abba*.

If we fail to think about ourselves
 in this way,
 then we will fail to hear God speak.
If we begin to believe somehow
 that we are our own source,
 that we establish our own destiny,
 that we are in control of life and death,
 then we will not hear,
 and the Self
  will not host *Abba*.
Then the Self is not open
 but closed,
 clinging as tightly as a clenched fist
  to shallow truths.
Then, too, if we hold back any part
 of our Self in our posture toward God,
 we will not hear God speaking.
If we withhold a memory,
 a hurt,

a pain,
a failure,
a desire,
a gift,
or any part of the Self,
we are blocking God's presence.
If we fail to admit our truth,
to accept our Self
then we are also blocked
from hearing God.
And what is truth?
It is the ever-unfolding grace
which shapes our lives.
It is the inner power to discover
over and over again
who we really are,
even when who we are
does not match very well
with culture or church.
There is open before us a vast horizon
of possibilities with God.
Like the great primeval beast
who dared not venture
out of the safety and shadows
of the forest
into that sunlit savannah,
we stand at the edge of the meadow now,
wanting to run free
in the Spirit's fresh breezes
yet fearing that very thing.
We see before us the freedom
of God's horizon,
larger, more inviting than our own,
and yet we hold back,
keep it inside,

hide carefully, and try to go on with our lives
the best we can.

And let it be said openly here
that we are free to do that.
We are free to see ourselves with God
or to withhold from God
whatever we will.
We are free to repress or suppress
any part of our Self.
Some of us will need help to open our lives
and hearts
to God.
Some may even require therapy
to open the Self,
to allow the Self to be transformed.
The healing process may not be easy
or the journey sweet.
But always we know
that union with *Abba*,
the union that Jesus makes possible now,
awaits us.

Reflect

How do you hear God speaking in your life?
Who are the people you have known who
seem to be most centered on their inner voices,
on God's presence?

3

~~

Hearing in the Silence

Whenever there is silence around us
    we can pause
    to hear the voice of God.
But silence is not easy to find
    these days
    and even when we find it
    it's not easy to tolerate
        in our busy lives.
Silence is dangerous for us
    if we want to avoid the truth
    because the moment we allow ourselves
    to fall silent,
        the truth wells up within us
        and nourishes us.
But such nourishment can make us
    uncomfortable
    and uneasy.

Despite our desire for it,
>we prefer the noisy clang of chatter
>>and music
>>and television
>>and anything else we can find
>>to avoid the disturbing moments of silence
>>in which we are confronted
>>with ourselves.
Silence, we should note,
>is more the norm than noise,
>however.
Words rise out of silence
>and return to it again
>leaving their insights
>>or hurt
>>or kindness
>>or sting behind them.
We live in silence
>except when we fill it with noise.

It seems to have been in the silence
>of his life
>that Jesus heard God's voice
>>most clearly.
In the quiet of the desert,
>pondering his own calling,
>sorting through the events of life
>>up to that point,
>he learned what it means to be
>>a child of God.
In the quiet moments just before
>inviting those who would follow him,
>thinking of his emerging work,
>he carefully considered the Word.

In the garden before his death,
   gripping with conviction
   a vision once seen,
      he expressed to *Abba* the fears
      that must have filled him.

Jesus was united to *Abba*
   so intimately
   that to know one
      was to know the other.
We, too, are united to God
   in this intimate way.
We share with Jesus
   a union of divinity and humanity
   in our very depths
   where God is found.
The light of this presence
   is so near,
   so ready to be encountered,
   that we need only pause
      and allow God to be present.
This prayerful encounter with *Abba*
   is the source of our spirit
   and the goal of our living.
But what is this encounter like for us?
   How do we know the truth?

The story of the woman at the well
   in the gospel of John
   can help us gain an insight
      into what this means
      for us.
In this story

an image of the encounter with God
is unfolded
in which we are invited
to know ourselves deeply,
 to encounter the truth,
 to "drink of the living water,"
 and thereby know God as well.
This is a wonderful story
 full of imagery and symbolism
 and told with great force
 in this gospel.
Jesus and a woman of Samaria
 encounter one another
 at a well on the road north
 from Judea toward Galilee.
There they find life in one another
 and out of these moments
 they both find their lives changed.
Jesus begins: he is thirsty
 and asks her for a drink;
 she hesitates because the social customs
  of first-century Judaism
  don't allow Jews and Samaritans
  and Rabbis and Women
   to mix.
These customs were centuries old
 and fixed firmly in the culture
 but Jesus took a cavalier attitude
  toward all that,
  dispensing with it freely.
Such barriers,
 according to Jesus,
 have no place in God's reign.
Abba cannot be contained in such a way
 as this.

So their visit begins
    and the text of John
    provides a tidy summary
    of what must have gone on
        between them.
The context of this encounter
    is a relationship:
    a sharing of life and time,
    a sharing of stories and insights.
There are no social barriers,
    no customs,
    no rules,
    nothing to stop the encounter
        with God.
We learn as we read along
    in this story
    that the woman here has suffered
    in her attempts to live
        a satisfied life.
She's tried many things,
    many partners,
    to no avail.
She's drunk from a fountain
    that gave no relief;
    she was thirsty still.

Jesus tells her that he can give water
    that will satisfy her thirst
        forever.
"…whoever drinks of the water I shall give
    will never thirst again,"
    he tells her.
"The water I give

will become a spring,
welling up to eternal life!"

"Sir,"
    the woman says,
    "give me this water..."

And so Jesus does.
He helps her find,
    in her own story,
    the fragments of divine life
    from which a tapestry
        of unconditional love,
        of total acceptance,
        of unending forgiveness
            could be woven.
He leads her to her own dying,
    to admitting her truth,
    to owning her life,
    to facing the realities of failure
    and to accepting the possibility
        of life.
Because of this encounter with Jesus
    this woman learns the truth
    and the truth sets her free.
In short,
    they pause together
    and allow the energy of God
    to well up within them,
        the spring of living water.
Now, rather than the unsatisfying water
    of life outside the truth,
    which she'd been drinking for so long,

this woman drinks freely
from the waters of openness,
    honesty,
    love,
    and kindness.
She drinks with delight,
    despite the embarrassment
    despite the fear
    despite the pain of such an encounter.
She enters into a dying to self
    that gives her new life,
    an encounter with *Abba*.
By leading her to the truth
    this way
    Jesus introduces her to God.
This is a profound encounter,
    one we ache for,
    one we long for,
    one we must die for.
"God is spirit,"
    Jesus eventually tells this woman,
    "and those who worship God
    must worship in spirit and truth."

This is the story of the gospels,
    told over and over again.
This is the prodigal son in Luke
    returning to a loving parent,
    coming home to himself
    and delighting in new life.
This is the blind Bartimaeus in Mark
    throwing off the mantle of fear
    and following Jesus with new insight
    on the way to *Abba*.

This is Matthew's vineyard
    where everyone is paid in full
    despite the lateness
    of their arrival.
We are these prodigal children,
    we are these blind beggars,
    we are these latecomers
    to the reign of God.
And we can drink the living water still;
    we are welcome,
    all of us.
Because this is, in short,
    the paschal mystery.
It is the dying and rising of Jesus,
    which is our dying, too,
    our rising with him.
With him we enter the regions of darkness,
    the shadows of our life,
    the shadow side of life,
    where we drink a kind of water
    that finally quenches our thirst.
With him we enter those dark regions
    of our lives
    to face our truth.
Notice in the story at the well
    that it was never a matter
    of undoing the truth,
    or of rejecting the past,
    or of judgment.
It was only a matter of facing it,
    befriending it,
    admitting it.
The darkness of evil,
    like the light,
    is very near at all times.

The woman's experience was an encounter
    with the light
    that illumined the dark:
    there she was given "living water."
"Sir,"
    the woman said,
    "give me this water
    that I might never thirst again...."

In one of his poems
    Samuel Taylor Coleridge,
    the British poet,
    leads us to this point, too.
In "The Rime of the Ancient Mariner"
    a group of sailors sets out to sea
    with fair winds and good weather.
At first their sailing is without incident
    and their efforts are easy.
But then,
    because of the misdirected actions
    of one of the crew,
        the winds die
        and the ship cannot move.
It stands in the southern seas
    under a blazing sun
    and its sails droop helplessly.
The fresh water on board
    is quickly drunk by the sailors
    in the heat of the days of waiting,
    and soon there is no water left
        for them,
        no fresh water.
All is salty now,
    and even though they drink it

in their desperation,
it cannot quench their thirst.
Then the poet says,
describing both ship and life:

"Day after day, day after day,
We stuck, nor breath nor motion;
As idle as a painted ship
Upon a painted ocean.

"Water, water, every where,
And all the boards did shrink.
Water, water, every where,
Nor any drop to drink."

We are those sailors,
we are the woman at the well,
or the prodigal child,
or the blind Bartimaeus,
or the latecomers into the kingdom.
We drink the salt water
of lies and stealth,
broken promises and indifference,
greed, lust, and busyness.
We spend our days drinking water
that does not satisfy
when all along
the living water is right before us.
"...water, water, every where
nor any drop to drink."

So, like this woman at the well,

we pause with Jesus
to encounter ourselves
and thereby "hear" God speak to us.
Such pauses in life
can happen daily,
and will often include others.
The way to the heart of the Lord
is seldom traveled alone.
This pause might be with the sacraments,
maybe reconciliation or eucharist,
or perhaps in a story shared with others,
or maybe in the memory of a hero or saint,
or even a moment alone in meditation.
In our encounters with one another
we always have the opportunity
to encounter *Abba.*
Or we can choose to drink the salt water
that leaves us thirsty.
We can share our stories honestly,
or we can cover them up with lies.
We can lovingly share our sexuality
or enter into meaningless,
anonymous sex.
We can touch one another
or turn away.
We can share our money generously
or we can hoard it with greed.
We can include all others in our lives
or we can exclude those who are different.
We can build solidarity in our communities
or we can let hate splinter us.
We can busy ourselves with noise and activity
or we can pause to be present
to one another.
We can, in short,

drink the living water together
or we can drink the salt water alone.
We can offer one another an encounter
with Christ
that leads to the depths of *Abba*
or we can droop on salty seas.

"Whoever drinks of the water
that I shall give
will never thirst again...."

Reflect

What is the "salt water" in your life? What do you do instead of listening for God's "fresh water" voice?

4

~~

The Inner Voices

Almost everyone
    has the sense
    that there is some meaning
    to life,
        some purpose
        greater than ourselves.
There seems to be a built-in
    sense of direction,
    an inner life-force,
    a call to journey
        down our own,
        unique path.
We're called to be something,
    not just *any* something
    but something special,
    something to which each of us
        is individually called.

So we carry around inside ourselves
   this sense of "our thing,"
   this notion that
      we have a special place in life,
         our inner sense of self.
Sometimes this inner urging
   is unclear
   or we refuse to hear it
      but it remains within us:
      a vague but present drumbeat,
      a cadence always calling us nearer.
But almost everyone
   has also gotten the idea
   that this something special
      toward which we are heading
      is a "call" from somewhere
         outside ourselves,
         from some divine person
         who lives beyond the world.
It goes something like this
   in much of our thinking:
God, who is outside of us,
   calls each of us to some state in life,
   and our task,
      according to this thinking,
      is to figure out
      just exactly what it is God wants.
But here, you see,
   is the problem.
How are we supposed to know
   exactly what God wants
   when God is so distant,
      so removed,
      so oblique in giving us direction?
In trying to understand this,

we've put together an image
of God
that isn't too flattering.
God, for most people,
still sits in heaven,
sometimes involved,
most times not,
with our everyday lives.
If we figure out what God wants,
then there's a chance
God will be pleased,
which is good
because an angry God means trouble.
If we don't figure it out,
then we may reach death's door
and learn that
we've done it all wrong,
that God is not pleased,
and that we'll spend eternity
paying for this mistake.
But in any case,
God remains in heaven,
and we remain on earth,
trying to understand
what in heaven's name
God wants.
The thing we're called to in life,
that special something
we believe we should do,
appears,
under this notion of God,
to be something we guess at.
Our calling,
our vocation in life,
as Thomas Merton said,

seems like part of some great
supernatural lottery.
Everyone's name is in the hat,
and some will be picked for this
and some for that.
Lucky the ones who seem to know
what they were chosen
to do.
Hearing the voice of God
in discernment has often been linked
to these images and notions of God.
Under this plan
our hope in discernment
is to correctly figure out
what God wants.
This whole notion
of God calling us
from some distant heaven
to an unsure task on earth
is fundamentally faulty.
It's more a function of modern,
North American piety
than of the Scriptures.

Under this notion of God
and God's "desire" for us,
we spend our lives
meditating upon a mystery
that is perceived to be
entirely outside ourselves
and our experience.
It's as though
God could not appear
within our own lives,

within our own experience,
within our own world,
within our own hearts.
So we search outside ourselves
to know what we are called
to do and to be.
And in so searching,
we often pass by our own truth,
our own revelation,
our own hearts.
We miss ourselves
and in the end
we often miss God as well.
God is, after all,
in the flesh now:
Jesus is born: Emmanuel!
So God, you see,
is in this world
and in our lives.
We needn't search beyond the stars
for God.
Yahweh is near;
Christ is incarnate.
Learning to trust,
to have faith,
does not mean we must place ourselves
outside ourselves,
as it were.
We needn't look for the earthquakes,
the raging fires and floods,
the terrible night storms.
Yahweh and Christ
speak in tiny whispers
in our inner voices.
They speak from our individual

and collective
inner lives:
and they speak words
to lead us always home,
to lead us to ourselves.
Learning to hear that inner voice,
and the direction it sets
for our lives,
is learning to hear God.
Listening to our lives,
directed toward the mystery
from which we come,
directed toward the inner longing
for the artist who made us,
is listening to God.
Having faith in that voice,
is having faith in God.
Trusting this direction
is trusting God.

This is not a listening
with our ears
or a seeing with our eyes.
It's not a believing based on proof,
or a trusting based on certainty.
It's not a sitting down once and for all
and coming away
with some sure sense
of who we are to be.
It's not a thinking at all.
Rather,
it's a looking into the stuff
of our lives,
a daily examination of our dreams,

our self-imagination,
our hopes,
our urges and aches,
our interests and yearnings.
In that stuff
we will find the makings
of our lives,
mysterious though that will be.
Mystery will always be part
of our discoveries there;
mystery will be our guide.
This is a listening
that requires of us
a brutal honesty.
It's a listening that will lead us
away from alienation,
separation,
polarization,
isolation,
and into our own hearts.
There we will find out that
connection,
compassion,
community,
and companionship
are possible after all.
We will find
when we listen to this inner voice
our Self there.
We will find a Self,
not centered on self,
but centered on the community
in which we live
and on the Mystery
from which we spring.

We will find a yearning for love,
   for open hearts,
   for kindness,
   for honesty,
   for full human living.
We will find a way to peace,
     to care for the earth,
     to gentleness with others,
     to an open spirit.
We will find within ourselves
   Mother and Father,
   the womb and the seed.
We are created
   toward such an end.
Knowing it and finding it
   and living it
   is pure bliss for us.

Jesus Christ,
   whose own encounter with discernment
   led him inexorably to *Abba*,
   his source and destiny,
     has made it possible for us
     to also know our hearts.
But the voice that calls us
   does not come from a cloud.
The skies will not open for most of us.
We will know our pathway
   when we follow our hearts
     and our intuitions.
When we do the thing
   that we know deep inside
   is right for us,
     then consolation is ours

and we are on our way.
When we can know this clearly,
    when we have the inner sense of what is right,
    then we must stay with it.
We must not let anyone throw us off
    even if at first
    others scoff
    and we appear to be foolish.
After all,
    Abraham and Sarah,
    Moses and Miriam,
    and Mary and Joseph
    did very "foolish" things.

We carry within us, then, a mysterious inner force
    for life and love,
    an ache for the truth,
    and an indivisible link to
        creation and creator.
Our lives are ordered toward this end
    and there's little we can do
    but discover that within ourselves.
The specific work we do,
    the specific people we love,
    the specific stuff of our lives
        all take their origin
        and root in this human condition.
It's the code of life for us.
Christ urges us to seek
    that inner sense of calling
    which is where God reigns.
This is not some heaven
    light years away;
    it's the real thing within us,

the thing we most urgently seek
the ache in our hearts
the thing we know deep down
that nobody can deny.
This is not a vocation
from a distant god
at which we must guess;
it's a movement within us
directed by a living God
pulling us toward ourselves
toward our Self:
a self-for-others
for peace
for harmony
in short, a self-for-God.

Even disasters in life
can be moments of hearing
this call.
Sometimes, in fact,
apparent disasters are the stuff
of which grace itself is made:
a new course is charted,
a new life begun.
In fact,
disasters in life:
divorce
death
losing a job
empty nesting
illness
fire
accidents
"being discovered"

might well be wonderful opportunities
    to begin again,
    inner urgings toward a truer life
    toward rising from ashes.

Many people live their entire lives
    without following their inner call.
They never do that thing
    which is most "them,"
    never follow their heart.
In their thinking,
    they're being responsible adults,
    doing the work expected of them,
        earning a living,
        making a name,
        caring for others,
        obeying the rules,
        perfecting the world,
        running the ship,
        keeping things tidy.
And so these people
    never know the bliss
    of following their yearning,
    listening to their ache,
    doing their real thing in life.
Some will wake up ten years into a job
    and find that they hate it,
    that they never liked it,
    but they stay there nonetheless.
Others study in college and trade schools,
    or enter a line of work in their youth
    and believe somehow
    that they must never vary from this course,
        that they must stay there forever.

Staying seems so easy
    while leaving means risk;
    other people might think they're unstable,
    they might not know where to go,
    habits and patterns in their lives
        might have to change.
So, staying, even in something they hate,
    is chosen over living
    according to their inner direction.

How very sad,
    because when we listen closely
    to that deep, inner voice,
    and follow our real route,
        then the world, too, prospers
        because all of us are living
        according to our *created* purpose.
Each of us can do the thing
    we most want to do in life
    which is to say that each of us can live
        in the reign of God,
    each of us can follow the pillar of fire
        in the night,
    each of us can learn to trust our inner voice.
And if each of us did,
    there would be no violence,
    no exclusions,
    no hatred,
    no darkness at all.
The light for which the world waits
    is not coming from above the stars
    but from within our human selves.
This light will come
    when the energy of God

flows through us,
when the world sees in us
what the world saw in Christ.
"If everyone lit
just one little candle,
what a bright world this would be!"

Reflect

What does your inner voice prompt you toward? When you pause to listen, what do you hear deep inside you?

5

~~

The Outer Voices

We're created to live in paradise,
    nothing less.
That's the original plan,
    according to the Hebrew
    and Christian Scriptures.
Paradise: a place of total bliss,
    our created purpose,
    what God originally intended.
Under this plan,
    from the beginning,
    everything and everyone
    lives out its intended purpose
        in harmony,
        peace,
        mutuality,
        and with the energy of love.
The fact that,

despite this excellent plan,
we do not live in paradise
is the subject of this chapter.
Given the beauty and loveliness
of paradise,
and given our natural longing
to be there,
what keeps us from doing it?
What prevents us from living
as we're intended to live?
Why can't we hear God's voice
more clearly?
We're going to look into that
a little here,
but first a pause
to remember our Story:
Christians and Jews have an account
of creation,
not unlike the stories of many others,
ancient and modern people alike,
who want to know the meaning
of life.
In fact, Jews and Christians
have more than one version
of the creation story
and both are included
in the first part
of the Book of Genesis.
These versions vary significantly
from one another
in giving the details
of the creation process.
But that's no problem for us,
because we know these stories
are not meant to give us facts.

They're meant to give us meaning,
  to help us understand life
    and God
    and ourselves
    and one another.
That's what mythology does:
  it tells a story to explain something
  for which the facts are simply unavailable.
The function of these stories
  is to awaken and stimulate
    a sense of wonder
    participation
    and awe
  in the mystery of our universe
  which we'll never really understand completely.
The Jewish and Christian creation stories
  are therefore true,
  but they're true about *us*,
    not about Adam and Eve.
What those stories tell us
  about ourselves and our world
  is that everything in creation
  exists in a balance
    with something else.
So light and darkness
  balance one another.
Good and evil exist side by side;
  male and female co-exist and co-create.
The earth itself is in a similar balance:
  a divine ecology
  under our stewardship.
This balance is vital for life
    peace
    harmony

understanding
and the survival of the earth.
It provides the setting
for all our understanding about God.
In fact,
being out of this balance
is clearly the cause of pain,
suffering,
killing,
poverty
and death.

In looking further at this,
to try to understand more deeply,
we could say that the people
in the story,
Adam and Eve,
are a lot like us.
They just wanted to live their lives,
and they were given
a place to do that.
They went along from day to day,
collecting food,
enjoying one another,
living in harmony,
not having to worry about much:
paradise!
In this living,
they knew they could trust
their inner sense,
because they often walked
with God
in the garden.
Walking with their artist,

with their gardener,
    formed their lives.
  They were walking, in other words,
    with their inner voice which is from God.
    This gave them a sense of self,
    an in-born knowledge,
      intuition,
      and imagination:
      a knowing-deep-down-what's-true.
We all have that inner voice,
    that inner sense of truth.
We can all hear it,
    trust it,
    feel it.
The energy of God,
    the force of love,
    flows through that voice
      to us.
It is an energy within us
    and all around us.
    It fills the earth
      and the universe.
In giving his sense
    of who Christ is,
    Saint Paul says in one place
      that Christ is the Force,
      the energy:
He is what holds the world together.

And this power
    "lets us" hear ourselves,
    our inner selves.
It's a voice of truth,
    of great love

of shameless nakedness,
of life itself.
Because, as the story goes,
they lived without shame and doubt
in their garden,
their paradise.
And as long as they trusted
their inner voice,
where God spoke to them,
they knew their way.

But then disaster!

Like all creation stories,
this one works hard to inform us
about life
and love
and ourselves.
None of the details in this story
are accidental.
The nature of their painful journey
to the dark side
is one of those details.
Let's look at it more closely.
At some point along the way,
the people in the story
began to trust in something
or someone
other than their inner voice
where they knew God.
It was this new trust
that did them in.
Reading closely,

you will see
that it was an "outer voice"
that got them in trouble.
Trusting someone else's voice:
for the woman, the serpent,
for the man, another person.
Both of them abandoned their inner voice,
and accepted the word
of someone outside themselves.
A close inspection of these texts
convinces us that it does not matter
where this outer voice originates,
but only that it was just that:
an *outer* voice.
What matters in this story
is that we learn from it
that we have a great power within us
to be what we're created to be.
This power flows through us
like a great river,
which we have only to trust,
only to follow faithfully.
It's the Force of Life,
the Power of Love,
the Word of Truth,
the Light of the World.
But when we give that power
to someone or something outside of us
then we fail to live
our full lives.

This outer voice, then,
famously incarnated in a serpent,
falsely promised them

that they would not die
if they trusted it.
It falsely promised them
that they would be like God,
like their artist,
their gardener,
their creator.
And it falsely promised them
that they would know more:
in particular the difference
between good and evil.
It promised,
in short,
a life of false paradise!
And as soon as they began to trust
this outer voice,
as soon as they gave away
their personal power to live,
they had shame,
and they wanted to hide.
For the first time they experienced
fear
anger
aggression.
They had begun the journey to the dark side
following,
not the voice of their artist,
but the outer voice of darkness.

And then what happened?
Well, as the story goes,
God was walking in the garden
in the cool of the evening.
The inner voice,

in other words,
was still very close,
and by the end of the day
they recognized it there.
But they hid from it,
hid from their maker.
(How can a work of beauty
hide from its own artist?)
Really,
they were hiding
from themselves.
They'd lost their true sense of self
which emerges from within:
a created sense,
a having-been-made-to-listen,
a this-is-really-who-I-am sense.
"Where are you?"
God called to them.
But they hid;
they heard their inner voice,
but having yielded
to the dark side,
they now feared it.
Anger, fear, and aggression
appear as soon as we move
to the dark side of the Force.

And when they finally stood there
aware of their awful choice,
they naturally blamed
the outer voice
from whom the trouble started.
"The serpent made me do it."
"She made me do it."

I think we can draw
an important conclusion
from this story.
Any outer voice that calls us
away from our created selves,
away from paradise,
away from our inner voice,
our walking with God
in the garden,
that voice is calling us to the dark side.
If we follow it,
we will not find our true way.
Jesus is the "new Adam, the new Eve."
We say that because he is Word,
not the word of the serpent,
but the Word of God.
Following this Word
hearing this voice,
will lead us home again,
will lead us back to our inner voice,
breathed into us on the shores
of that great river
at the moment of our creation.

We began by saying here
that this is a story about us.
It gets uncomfortable for us
to admit this
and deal with it,
because it's so true.
We are surrounded by outer voices
that tempt us
to the dark side
every day of our lives.

What is advertising
    if not such an outer voice?
It promises us paradise,
    advertising does;
      it promises that we will not die,
        that we will be like God,
        that we will understand more.
And it is everywhere today:
    television
    newspapers
    breakfast cereal boxes
    church bulletins
    billboards.
It bombards us with a kind of warfare
    in which we must be very strong
    not to be overwhelmed by it.

Now let me pause to clarify
    that advertising as an outer voice
    is not by its very nature
    on the dark side.
In many small communities,
    it is simply the way people learn
    about what's available in town.
In many larger communities,
    advertising simply functions
    to make known the availability
      of services and products
      in a neighborhood.
That kind of advertising is helpful
    and kind.
But there is a more insidious kind
    that creates needs
    in order to sell products.

This kind is dangerous,
    manipulative,
    clever,
    and common.
This is true especially for children,
    but for all of us as well.
In most Western cultures
    and much of the Third World
    this kind of advertising is so dominant
    that it's really out of control.

Listen to children during the holidays
    when gift-giving is the custom.
How do they know what they want?
    They have been told by an outer voice
        what will make them smart,
        or popular
        or important
        or happy!
Imagine this!
We've developed a system of outer voices
    that worms its way into us
        and our children
        and confuses our very selves.
Their inner voices
    will not lead them to the latest fad
    but to trust
        honesty
        beauty
        intimacy
        and simplicity.
Our children believe that the outer voice
    calls them to happiness:
    "If only I had this or that,

then I would be happy,"
they will tell us.
But they've been lied to by the serpent
and if they follow the lie,
they will become people of the lie,
just as many of us have.

Evil it is, then,
when we allow this outer voice
to silence our inner sense
of truth
and goodness
and beauty.
So, for example,
the constant litany of advertising
for women's or men's beauty products
creates for many of us
the idea that we're ugly.
We don't have the right eye color,
or the right tan,
or the right skin.
The idea is that if we did have
everything right
then we would also be happy.
But it's all false.
Maybe we're aging,
or gaining weight
or wanting to live more simply,
but this outer voice
insists on its way:
we must act
or buy
or *live*
according to its call.

It's very difficult then
to trust our inner voice;
it may even be difficult to hear
that inner voice speak
because of all the outer voices
around us.
In order to really hear the voice of God
we must confront
the outer voices in our culture.
This advertising of which we speak here
is an essential part
of our total economic system.
In this system,
sales are its fuel;
"Nothing happens," the theory goes,
"until something is sold."
We see that many North Americans are well fed,
have adequate homes,
and good jobs
because of this system.
When we see television reports
about Eastern Europe,
South and Central America,
West Africa, Asia,
or our own cities,
we're grateful we don't live there
because the people look so poor.
We're grateful for our system
and defensive about its weaknesses
and unwilling to let go of our foothold
in the global economic picture.
But like the Hebrew people in Egypt,
we've grown so accustomed to this
that we've forgotten we are slaves.
We've been lulled into believing

that consumerism is a greater value
 than economic justice,
that material possessions matter more
 than charity,
that competition to be on top
 has more value than cooperation,
that individualism is more "manly"
 than sharing community.

This brings us naturally
 to a second outer voice
 that is related to the first: money.
Money talks!
 It's a clear voice in our lives
 that speaks more loudly than most others
 and that cleverly directs our choices.
It's the most insidious outer voice
 of all.
At this point, many of you
 will wag your heads
 and not go on.
 But know that you are not alone in this.
We are rarely willing
 to examine closely the role
 that financial security plays
 in our lives.
It's insidious because it's wormed
 its way into our lives
 so subtly and so completely
 that we really believe
 having money means being in paradise.
It's often the last corner
 of our lives
 we are willing to let go of.

It's the private,
    self-controlled,
    final refuge of our lives.
We trust money
    more than anything else,
    including God.
"Money can't buy happiness"
    the old saying goes.
But we really believe it can.

The Christian Scriptures
    have a great story about this.
Jesus is teaching one day
    and his followers are learning
    about trusting God:
        do not hate
        turn the other cheek
        love your enemies
        the first shall be last
        be childlike
        and so on.
There's a fellow standing
    in the background of this scene,
    not visible to the reader at first,
        but in the mind
        of the gospel writer
        he's there all along.
This guy's a little uncomfortable
    because there's a vague sense
    within him
        that something is missing
        in his life.
He's apparently been keeping the rules;
    but still there is a restlessness
    within him.

His search may have taken him
  to a variety of religious movements;
  he may have been asking around
    about his emptiness
    for some time.
Finally he ventures a question
  to Jesus:
  "Master," he asks,
    "what must I do to have
    eternal life?"
What a wonderful question!
  It's the one we're always asking.
Jesus knew the human heart well
  because his answer
  went to its core.
First he told him
  that he must follow the commandments
    of God.
I do that, said the man,
  and I have done so since my youth.
One more thing you must do, then,
  Jesus told him,
  you must stop allowing money
    to be your god.
You must order your financial life
  according to the plan of God.
If you follow money,
  then money will be what you have,
  but not paradise.
Jesus knew that this young man
  wasn't in touch
    with himself,
    with his own source
    with his true way.
He was following money instead.

"If you would be perfect,"
     Jesus said in the text,
     "go, sell what you possess
     and give to the poor,
     and you will have treasure
     in heaven;
          and come, follow me."
Look for your treasure in trusting me,
     in trusting God,
          he might have said.
Follow your inner voice:
     Don't let money rule your life.
     Don't think keeping the rules
          is enough.
Don't let any outer voice
     keep you away
     from your true call.
Well,
     as the story goes,
     the rich young man went away sad,
          shaking his head.
This was just too much to ask!
His search for paradise,
     for rest and comfort,
     for life and love,
          would continue.
But where else could he ever look?

A large portion of the moral sayings of Jesus
     in the gospel of Matthew
          deal with our addiction to greed.
Greed is a very real obstacle
     to hearing the voice of God,
          but it's an obstacle we refuse to acknowledge.

In Matthew's story of Jesus' birth,
    for example,
    there are no poor shepherds.
    (They appear only in Luke.)
In Matthew we have wise men,
    apparently wealthy ones,
    who come bringing gifts of great value:
    gold, frankincense, ointments.
They come, in a word,
    to share their resources,
    to give away their wealth.
Only Matthew takes pains to advise
    on giving alms
    and to warn:
        "Do not lay up for yourselves
        treasures on earth...."
Your heart and your treasure,
    he says later,
    will always be in the same place.
"You cannot serve both God and money...."

Matthew himself appears to have been
    a tax collector,
    a worker in the economic system
        of his day.
But he was called from that
    into a new community,
    a community of justice and charity.
Matthew's walk with Jesus
    seems to have awakened in him
    an ability to hear the voice of God
    beyond the din of economic noise.
So, for us to really hear the voice of God,
    we must confront the false god, money,

and confront it squarely.

Let's talk about another voice now,
   one that is more troublesome
   and more difficult to explore:
      Christian religion.
Christian religion today is caught
   between wanting to urge people
   to trust their inner voices
      where God speaks,
      on the one hand,
   and insisting upon its own rules,
   which function as an outer voice
      in people's lives,
      on the other.
It appears that for some religious leaders
   fidelity is understood
   as a mere following of rules,
      the outer rules of The Law.
"You can't find the truth
   within yourself,"
   this definition of religion goes,
   "you can only find it
      by obeying the church."
I'm sure these leaders don't mean
   to contradict Jesus
   who insisted that merely keeping the law
   is not enough.
I'm sure these leaders would be the last
   to argue that fulfilling
      a minimal obligation
      is sufficient to meet
      the real demands of the gospel.
I'm sure they mean to say
   that Christians are to regard the law

as a starting point,
a guide,
a way to inform their own decisions.
I'm sure these church leaders
would never suggest that one's conscience
is not more important than the law.

The ultimate and first goal
of the Christian churches
is to provide a community context
which will be a guide
to people who are following Jesus Christ.
The preaching and education
that these churches provide
is meant, it seems,
to inform the inner lives
of the faithful,
to help the faithful know Christ,
which is to know the light,
to be enlightened,
to be full of grace.
In short, it is to help people
identify in their own lives
the experience of the divine energy there
and, having identified it,
allow it to form them,
direct their shared worship,
and reconcile them and the world.
But when the churches
get a little nervous
about people following their inner call,
trusting their inner voice,
being directed by their own consciences,
they tend to come down hard

with rules and regulations
that the faithful must keep
in order to be considered
worthy of eternal life.

The rules and regulations
that church leaders sometimes impose,
are intended to inform the heart,
to form the inner voice
of the followers.
But sometimes they function only
as outer voices.
The reasons for this are many
but may have more to do with style
than content.
You see,
Christ must be born within us,
the law must be written
on our hearts.
It is never enough
to have blind obedience
to the letter of the law.
If all we do is to externally
fulfill some minimal obligations,
then we've lost our way.
Religion has failed
to inform our inner voice,
our conscience.
It has succumbed
by noisily shouting about rules,
and it has become an outer voice.
And whether you believe in Christ,
or Buddha,
or Yahweh,
it's the same goal.

Religion must be read in terms
of an inner life,
shared in community,
and leading to paradise.
Anything else isn't really religion.

We repeat the story of the garden
again and again.
Hebrew prophets knew this
and urged the people
to write the law upon their hearts.
Jesus himself seemed quite cavalier
about following the rules,
preferring to re-understand them
in light of his unity with *Abba*,
in light of his inner voice,
in light of love.
Jesus knew that it is quite possible
to follow all the rules
and yet have hearts of stone
when it comes to love,
to living in paradise.

In conclusion,
let's review a bit what we've done.
We've examined three obstacles
to hearing the inner voice:
Advertising
Money
and
Religion.
We've talked briefly about these three outer voices,
which sometimes keep us
from really hearing the voice of God.

There are, of course,
    many more than three.
We have not examined the role of propaganda
    that our government
    and other governments
        use to convince people
        regarding national ideologies.
We have not thought about educational systems
    that focus students on approaches
        to philosophy
        history
        economics
        agriculture
        business
        teaching
        or other fields
    without freeing them to take unique
    approaches that differ
    from the status quo.
We have not discussed the inner,
    psychological person
    where many obstacles may be found:
        authority confusion
        perfectionism
        sexual ambivalence
        asocial behaviors
        depression
        withdrawal.

And there are still other factors
    that are obstacles
    to hearing God's voice.
We live in complex modern times
    with many voices competing

for our hearts and minds.
Discerning among them,
    seeking healing,
        freedom,
        and peace
    is a life-long journey.
In this journey
    we need to cling to one another
    for guidance.
We find one another as community
    as church
    as companion
        and we conspire together.
The word conspiracy
    is a good one.
It originates from two Latin words:
    con and *spirare*
    meaning literally,
        to "breathe together,"
        to con-spire,
            to share the Spirit.
At the beginning of Vatican II
    the new spirit was called "fresh air,"
    in Italian, *aggiornamento,*
    a throwing open of the windows.
Now we must be open to this again.
We who seek the voice of the living God
    in the din of our culture and times,
    must conspire together to do so.
We will not find the way alone
    and we will not find it
    by looking to outer voices
        to inform us.
We will find it by looking within
    and sharing that inner journey

in a community of faithful people
committed to being together in life.
We conspire with these companions of ours,
conspire to seek ways to really live
amid the noisy din
of modern life.
A fresh breeze will blow into our lives
when we do this,
when we cease allowing outer voices
to so dominate our lives
that we cannot hear
the voice of God within.
We will breathe this fresh breeze,
this new *aggiornamento,*
and we will breathe it together
as conspirators.

Nikos Kanzantzakis might be our herald
because he wrote:
"And I strive to discover
how to signal my companions...
to say in time a simple word,
a password,
like conspirators.
Let us unite,
let us hold each other tightly,
let us merge our hearts,
let us create for Earth
a brain
and a heart,
let us give a human meaning
to the superhuman struggle."

Reflect
What outer voices distract you from "hearing
the voice" of God?

6

~~

Paying the Price

"There's no such thing
   as cheap prayer..."
   to paraphrase
   both Bonhoeffer and Friedman.

Following your true way in life,
   listening closely to God's voice,
   is going to cost you something.
There will be trade-offs
   with which you should be familiar
   because most people,
      when they see the cost,
      back away in fear.
I'm afraid the cost for some
   may be very great.
But the rewards are much greater
   for any who choose

to respond to this call,
to hear this inner voice,
in a word,
to follow their hearts.

What will these costs be?
Every person who makes the choice
to follow the inner voice
will undergo both death and birth.
Death is never cheap,
and birth is never without pain.
Christians will recognize
the Paschal Mystery in this:
death leading to life.
Jews will remember the Passover,
the Reed Sea,
and the Desert,
that led to a Promised Land.
Religious storytellers
from all parts of the earth
have known this mystery:
death and birth have a price.
So hearing God's voice costs us something
and we want to examine
some of those costs here.

The first cost is certainty.
We want to be certain about our lives
and the people around us.
We want to be sure
they will like us,
care for us,
include us.

We want our jobs to be sure,
    no changes,
    no threats,
    no insecurity.
We want to know where we'll be
    next year,
    next month,
    tomorrow.
We want to know ourselves,
    our interests,
    our yearnings,
    our urges,
    and our inner life.

But when we allow ourselves
    to get mixed up
    with following an inner leadership,
        rather than an outer one,
        all of this is up for grabs.
We've made a science of certainty,
    but all of us know,
    deep inside,
    that nothing is really sure,
        except change.

Still we cling to certainty
    even when we aren't happy.
Many of us get to a point
    in our lives
    where we look around and wonder
        why we're not satisfied
        with the place we're in.
Many of us realize after great struggle

that the relationships
we hoped to enjoy
have been killing us.
Many of us sense that something
is missing in our lives,
something vague
and barely identifiable.
Many of us wonder,
after all these years
of reciting our creed,
whether we really believe,
or whether belief really matters.
We've professed belief
in Yahweh or Christ,
in the Bible or the church,
in someone's teachings;
but have we ever believed
in ourselves?
Many of us know
that we've lived our whole lives
up to this point,
without ever really doing
the thing we most want to do.
We've never written our stories and songs,
never cried about that pain,
never loved that man or woman,
never took that trip,
never told someone about our love,
our hate,
our fear and longing.
We've never followed
our own intuition,
but have followed instead
some outer law,
some outer voice,

someone or something outside
our very selves that promised certainty.
We've never trusted our imagination,
never shared our story,
never really let anyone know us,
really *know* us.

But it's never too late
to trust our inner voice.
It doesn't matter
whether we're rich or poor,
living in Harlem or Sioux Falls.
It doesn't matter
what we do for a living
or where we have been.
It doesn't matter
what choices we have made
up to this point,
what mistakes,
what errors in judgment,
what wrong turns.
It's never too late
to trust the voice of the Creator
humming away inside us.
This is a truth
that we know deep inside:
we can always return
to our created selves,
we can always go home.
But in order to do so,
we have to be willing to pay the price,
that awful price:
We have to give up our certainty,
the false beliefs we've befriended,

gotten comfortable with,
and lived with for so many years.
"I set before you
life and death,"
Yahweh told the people:
"Choose Life!"
But so often we find
that we've lived in a place
of death-dealing narrow choices
for so long
that we are no longer able
to leave the security of death
for the uncertainty of life!

The second cost
is similar to the first:
It is familiarity.
We have to take off the tie,
or the apron
or the collar
or the overalls
and move on.
At first,
when we recognize what we must do
and begin to move in that direction,
it will feel violent.
We will pull up roots
sever ties,
begin a journey whose end
we can barely perceive
and whose beginning
we can barely believe.
We will see as we go
other roads,

other paths,
other ways we might have gone.
We will see places to escape;
but we will know
there is no turning back.
There will be deep mystery in this,
a form of aloneness
from which no one can escape,
a sense of self,
both sure and vague,
that individuates.
The familiar will yield
to the new
and the new will leave us,
initially,
uncomfortable:
with Christ on a cross
with Yahweh in the desert.
The violence of this beginning,
of the first steps in the journey,
will make us shrink in fear
because we love familiarity.
The truth,
we are told,
will set us free
but the way to freedom
may separate us
from those who hate the truth.
Friends will wonder
when they see us.
"What happened?" they will ask,
"you used to be so normal."
"What are you up to now?" they will wonder,
wagging their heads;
"you used to be so predictable."

The truth may separate
    father from son,
      mother from daughter.
It may make some turn in disgust,
    while others will wonder
    where you find the strength
      for so much freedom.

When you follow your true calling,
    leaving certainty and familiarity
    behind you,
    you will also encounter another cost:
      enslavement.
We are called to be free;
    but many of us
    can't imagine what that means.
We have befriended
    what enslaves us.

Some of us are enslaved in hiding:
    No one really knows who we are;
    we may never have revealed
      our deepest Self.
For some of us to come out of hiding
    would mean accepting the light,
    accepting ourselves,
    asking others to accept us.
There is so much risk in this
    that many of us will simply
    continue to hide.
But hiding is a step
    down the dark path
      of fear

repression
and self-hatred.
We hide in the shadows of life.
In the story of the Garden,
   we hid ourselves in shame
   because we trusted that outer voice.
We are not following our true call
   when we hide like this.

Others are enslaved
   by accepting the status quo.
The civil rights movement in the U.S.
   took its heart from one woman
   who would no longer sit
   in the back of the bus,
      who would no longer accept
      her enslavement,
      no longer live with the status quo.
The status quo is so comfortable
   for us
   so safe, so easy.
We know the cost of breaking out of that:
   It can be terribly high.
      It can even be death.

Many are enslaved
   by commitments badly made;
   for them, it is more important
      to be "right"
      than to be loving and free.
We live
   with such limited freedom
   that we are not always able to give

full consent
in committing ourselves to others.
When freedom finally rings
in our lives,
some commitments may change.
Rather than treating that as failure,
can we consider it growth?
Can we offer one another
understanding
rather than judgment
about such growth?
Is it better to remain in a commitment
badly made and enslaving
than to move on from mistakes
and live in the light?

Some are enslaved
by the rules of others,
as though keeping a rule
would make one a full person,
as though it might not be necessary
for the "rules" to be written
upon our hearts.
Some of these rules
were set by our parents
or pastors,
or teachers.
But are they truly our own?
At some point in our lives,
we need to sit down with ourselves
and examine those
unwritten rules
that govern us.

Most of us are enslaved
　　by a fear of dying;
　　we are afraid to end a life
　　　　that we have never fully lived.
We have so many regrets
　　when we haven't followed our inner voice,
　　that we hope
　　　　we can outlive ourselves!
But once we've begun
　　to allow the Force of Life
　　to flow through our journey
　　　　we come to understand that death
　　　　is part of life
　　and that we really haven't lived
　　until we've died!

We pass in death
　　to the other side,
　　not the dark side
　　　　but the place of light.
Eternity has already begun now and
　　we are already living
　　an "eternal life."
The patterns of our lives now
　　are the patterns we follow forever.
If the patterns we choose now
　　are faithful to our inner voice,
　　we will experience paradise.
But when we know
　　we haven't chosen the way of truth
　　in life,
　　　　we fear death.
Death then becomes darkness
　　because we know

our time of choosing is over.

In sum,
    the price we will pay
    for the bliss of living freely
        will be great.
We have to let go of our certainty,
    our control,
    our predictability,
    our familiarity,
    our comfortable enslavement.
To do this we may have to alienate a parent,
    or a child,
    or someone else.
We may have to separate ourselves
    from friends and family.
We may have to "break the rules"
    to venture into the unknown,
    to place our security,
        our stories,
        our poetry,
        our gentleness,
        our peace,
        or even our lives on the line.
Sometimes we won't know where we are going,
    not exactly,
    but we won't need to.
For when we follow our true calling,
    as Joseph Campbell points out,
    we put ourselves on a track
        that has been there
        all the while,
        waiting for us,
    and the life we ought to be living
        is the one we will be living.

In conclusion we could say
    that when we hear the voice of God
    and shape our lives
    by what we hear,
        there will be for us,
        as there was for Jesus,
        a tremendous price to pay.
The cost indeed is great
    when we follow our true call,
    but what we get in return
        is out of this world!

Reflect
What would it cost you to begin listening to
your own inner voice and following it?

7

~~

The Dark Side

With all this focus
    on fulfillment and happiness,
    you must be wondering
        about this question:
Isn't following your own way,
    listening to your inner voice,
    hearing God speak in your life,
        a selfish thing to do?
Isn't it possibly a step
    very near the dark side?

To answer this serious question,
    we must look carefully
    at the dark side itself.
This won't be an easy examination;
    speaking of darkness never is.
It isn't that the dark side
    is stronger than the light;
    it is not!

But it is subtle,
   close,
   within us,
   as near as the light.
The flow of darkness into our lives
   can begin as easily
   as a raised voice,
      a defensive gesture,
      a tiny lie,
      a suspicious eye.
Learning to feel the Force,
   to live in the Light of Christ,
   to know Yahweh
   to be at one,
      atoned,
   is a lifelong task.
It is always like walking through a forest
   with the darkness all about;
   it's so easy to step off the path.
One turn of the head,
   one quick thought,
   one moment's pause,
      and the dark side of the Force
      is there.

We've been using this term,
   describing the dark path,
   speaking of darkness,
   and always in contrast to light,
   to The Light.
Its use here
   is borrowed from religious writers.
In one of the creation stories
   of the Hebrew and Christian people,

God is said to have created
light on the first day.
"And God said,
'Let there be light'
and there was light...
and God separated
the light from the darkness."
But, and this raises the question for us,
the sun and moon weren't created
until the *fourth* day
in this story.
So what is this light about
on the first day?
And what is the darkness?
Is it simply the storyteller's
chronological mistake?
Or is there some connection
between this light
and the burning bush,
the pillar of fire leading
the Hebrew people
in the night desert,
and the coal that cleansed
the lips of the prophet?
Christians learn of Christ,
the light of the world,
a light no darkness can overcome.
In the teachings of Jesus,
his followers are themselves
called to be light:
"You are the light of the world,"
Jesus says.
"Let your light shine before all
that they may see your goodness
and give glory

to the Creator
who is in heaven."

Zen Buddhists speak of being en*light*ened,
    of coming into the light,
    as it were.
An enlightened one,
    according to one Zen Master,
    has accomplished emancipation
       and attained eternal peace.

There's been a lot of talk,
    then,
    about light and darkness.
We must understand these
    as two sides of the same coin,
    two dimensions of reality.
It isn't that we would want one,
    or could have one,
    without the other.
The dark side
    is the dark side of the light,
    of the life force.
It isn't that we are to be
    all light
    with no darkness at all,
       but rather that we are
       to know the dark,
       even wrestle with it,
    but remain in the light.
The prologue to John's gospel
    in the Christian Scriptures
    does not say that Christ

would drive out the darkness.
On the contrary,
 Christ is announced as the light
 that shines *within* the darkness
 and the darkness has not overcome it.
A few verses later,
 in the same Prologue,
 Christ is called the true light
 that enlightens every person,
  echoing Zen.

Balance is the goal,
 dialogue with the darkness,
 awareness,
 caution,
  knowledge of darkness,
  but not denial.
There is great spiritual agreement
 among world religions today
 about the meaning of this.
We can know
 when we are in the light,
 according to this unspoken consensus.
It is when we are full of compassion,
  careful with one another,
  in harmony with mother earth,
  giving of ourselves,
  sharing our suffering,
  awake to love,
  and attentive to our hearts.
When our choices
 lead us any other way,
 even if we think it is to happiness,
 it is not.

Choices that are destructive of life
    are choices of darkness.
So following our true way
    when we understand it
        as part of the journey to enlightenment,
           is never selfish.
In fact, our journey will lead us
    in just the other direction.
Our created selves
    are not selves-for-self.
We are Self for others,
    for the earth,
    for union with the Creator,
    for bliss and paradise.
I have never known someone
    who could say to him or herself
    "This is really *me*,
        the me I'm created to be,
        the me I'm empowered to be"
    and then be destructive.
It's just the opposite:
    really being yourself,
    your created self,
    leads to paradise, not hell.
What leads to hell
    is not trusting
    that the Force is always with us,
        that Yahweh's covenant is forever,
        that Christ's reign is within,
        that Enlightenment is near.

There is a story,
    a disturbing story,
        that helps us understand this well.

It is *The Strange Case*
 of Dr. Jekyll and Mr. Hyde
 by Robert Louis Stevenson.
This story has been told and re-told
 many times,
  most recently by John Sanford
   and Barbara Hannah
   to help us understand
   the shadow side of reality.
In the story,
 a respected London resident,
  Dr. Jekyll,
 yields to a temptation
 to allow the dark side
 to dominate his destiny.
He's become aware
 of the potential in himself
 for cruelty,
  hatred,
  aggression,
  lust,
  and death,
  and he finds a mysterious attraction
  to these:
   a *desire* for them.
So he conceives a plan
 whereby he can enter this shadow,
 this dark side,
  but return to his respected self
  at will.
He develops a drug
 that allows him to do this,
 and he names his dark side
  Mr. Hyde.
When he takes the drug

his countenance changes
and he enters into the deeds
which as a Christian gentleman
    he would normally abhor.
He acts out the darkest deeds
    of his desire,
        doing the very things his real Self
            would never want to do.
Hyde is hideous,
    evil
    cruel
    and hated by all.
With this drug,
    Jekyll can move between his selves,
    dallying with the dark side
    but returning to the light.
For some time he plays around with this
        recklessly,
    allowing his dark side to dominate
        because he takes such a perverse joy
        in doing so.
Living on the dark side
    allows him sensual pleasures,
    selfish pursuits,
    destructive actions:
        all ways foreign to the light.
So in and out of the dark he goes,
    taking the drug
    to change himself
        and returning to his Jekyll self,
        to the light,
        when the night is over.
But soon he finds
    that he can no longer control so well
    his desire to return to the good self.

Soon he finds that
    his dallying with darkness
    has made it impossible for him
        to return to the light.
In horror,
    he realizes that he has *become*
    Mr. Hyde
    and he dies a tragic death
        under that guise.

This is a disturbing story
    because we know it describes
    the unconscious of our own lives.
The dark side is so near,
    and dallying with it,
    walking the dark path from time to time
    "just for the hell of it,"
        can lure us to living there.

The lesson seems clear:
    our deliberate decision
    to choose darkness
        tends to become fixed in us.
Our deliberate decisions
    not to live as we are created to live,
    not to follow the light,
    not to follow our true way,
        solidify in us
        an absorption into evil.
Ancients called this
    "satanic possession."
Saint Paul complained of doing the things
    he most did not want to do.

C.G. Jung spoke of us
becoming what we do.

For Dr. Jekyll,
the tension of carrying
both darkness and light within him
was overwhelming.
His mistake was in attempting
either to live out the deepest,
darkest desires of his shadow
or to attempt to separate himself
completely
from his dark side.
Neither will bring us to peace.
Neither is the answer.

For us it is
to balance within ourselves
the light and the dark,
denying neither
but living in the light.
For us it is
to know and understand
those dark inclinations
to which we're more inclined
but not to yield to them.
For us it is
to see set before us
life and death,
and to choose life.
For us it is
not to escape the tensions
of the pathway,

but to know the Force
is with us.
For us it is "a delicate criss-cross
of a thread
on which we all do hang";
it is called crucifixion.

Reflect
What are the greatest temptations to the dark side that you face in your life?

8

~~

Trust

The first step
    in learning to hear the voice of God
    is to trust.
We so often place our trust
    in what leads us
    away from our true selves,
    away from paradise,
    away from the created order
    and into misery,
        disappointment,
        dishonesty,
        dis-ease:
            the dark side
            of the Force.
These become like god to us
    and we believe in them
    steadfastly.
We are called

to get rid of this god
in order to enter into God.

But here's the beauty
of creation:
God hasn't breathed God's life into us
for nothing;
we have a spirit of clarity,
of truth,
of paradise
within us
that can never
be taken or given away,
completely.
We can learn to trust,
to concentrate,
to allow the Force of life
to flow through us.
We must listen carefully
for that inner voice
where God reveals our own intimate,
inseparable,
parental relationship to *Abba*.
For us, as for Jesus,
the trust is the same:
Abba is our nourishment.
Abba is the source of our power.
Abba is our destiny.
We are now children of God, too,
sons and daughters of the Living One.

This means (and we can barely believe this!)
that God speaks in our lives
just as clearly as in Jesus'.

Those who are learning to trust
  the voice of God
  are around us
  and are recognizable to us.
And as we ourselves begin
  to trust God
  we will also be called by others.
We will be called
  to provide unstructured
    and unforeseen availability
    as others journey by.
We will ourselves
  continually
  be journeying with them.
We may be called from our homes,
  as Abraham and Sarah were,
  and sent to new lands.
We may glimpse a burning bush
  and be afraid to walk on holy ground,
  and yet be asked to lead a people.
We may be called
  to witness in ways
  that leave us vulnerable,
    hated,
    misunderstood,
    even martyred.
We may be left hanging
  on that delicate criss-cross
  of tensions
    within other people's lives,
    within their broken dreams.

We may be called
  to let go of our rigidity,

to become supple;
or we may be called to
    structure our lives more clearly,
    to witness to orthodoxy
    in a moment of someone's doubt.
We may be called to allow others
    to see inside us,
    to witness our struggles,
        no matter how private,
        to reveal ourselves to others.
We may be asked
    to show the way,
    to model a life of prayer,
    to hold someone rocked with agony
        and despair
        who cannot trust at all.
We may be forced to change
    our very selves again and again
    to be more pure,
        more centered,
        more able to love others.
We may be asked
    to witness to our trust,
    to make clear the courage
        of our convictions,
    to reach into our depths
        and offer hospice to others.
We may be asked,
    in short,
    for the truth of our lives
    so that others might trust
        the truth of theirs.

There is no possibility
    that we can be harmed
    on this journey
        if we trust this way.
Dangerous as the perils are,
    near as the dark side is,
    narrow as the path winds,
    often as we wander astray,
        the light is with us
        when we trust
        our inner voice,
        our intuitions,
        our sense of truth,
        and our God.

Reflect

In what do you place your greatest trust?
When has your trust been misdirected?

9

~~

Dancing with Grace

Have you ever watched pairs of birds
    dancing in the sky?
They touch,
    circle,
    return and touch again.
Then they seem to disappear
    but just as quickly
        reappear,
        still dancing together.
Sometimes it seems to be a chase,
    sometimes a waltz,
    sometimes a race.
It appears playful,
    gentle,
    loving.
It would not occur to me
    that one of the birds would fly away
    and never return
        to the dance!

They are together
   and alone there would be no dance,
      no poetry,
      no birdly bliss.

In the end,
   our lives are a dance like that,
   a dance with God's grace.
Despite what the outer voices
   of our culture
   or religion
   or government
   or advertisers
      tell us:
         There is no corner on the market
            of grace.
In fact,
   there is no market.
Grace is elusive,
   poetic,
   awesome,
   uncontained.
It's a dance of love and life,
   a circling around
   and coming back,
      a moving in harmony
      and a race into the horizon.
We touch it,
   like a kiss,
   but we never own it.
We never own it, period.
The moment we try to corner grace,
   control it,
   sell it,

market it to others:
    Poof! It's gone!
It evades our grasp
    and yet it is so close at hand.

What is needed in order to have grace
    is maddeningly simple:
    we merely let go of our own controls,
        our own weak attempts
        to create it
        or force it upon ourselves.
We let down our defenses,
    relax,
    take a step back
        and follow the Call.

When we are attuned
    to Yahweh
    or to Christ,
        we know this is true.
We cannot create love:
    We can make no one love us.
This simple truth
    evades us.
We continually try
    to make ourselves lovable
    but to no avail
        because love is free;
        it cannot be made.
We likewise cannot create peace
    for ourselves.
    It comes like a gift,
        an outcome of living in truth.

We also cannot create happiness.
   Joy in life,
      that sense of well-being
         for which we ache,
         is elusive, too.
But joy will appear
      when we know we have chosen
      that in life
         which is most truly our own.
And these:
      this joy and peace and love
      together constitute our happiness.
Happiness is not fixed,
      static,
      unchanging.
It is not metered out by a product
      or a church
      or a government.
It sleeps in us,
      waiting always to emerge;
      and it will emerge if we let it.
There is a choreography in life
      that we discover
      as we learn to trust,
      as we move beyond obstacles,
      as we discover grace.
It's vibrant,
      on-going,
      evolving,
         like the earth itself.
It unfolds before our very eyes
      as doors open
      and people enter
      and our hearts fill.
And then it seems to disappear,

hidden behind our fears,
invisible in the dark side.
For a moment,
a great shining moment,
we hear God's voice so clearly,
and we hang on with stark conviction
to the truth of that.
But then again it seems to pass away
and we stand,
intently listening in silence,
wondering where and when
and how we heard it.
There seems to be no music now,
no uptake
no cadence.
But the rhythm of the dance continues
beneath the surface
and soon it reappears.
Sometimes the dance is Zorba
on the beach,
wild! crazy! vigorous!
Sometimes it's two people dancing
cheek-to-cheek
in life and sex and love.
Other times the dance
is a circle,
women and men joined
arm in arm,
dancing life into each other,
drawing the energy of the earth,
sharing solidarity or eucharist.

For our part, we need these things
to learn this dance of life,

this dance of grace:
>   to hear the inner music,
>   to let it move us,
>   and to follow its rhythms.

Let the dance begin!

Reflect

As you complete this book, what feelings and hopes emerge in you? What change do you want? What affirmation did this reading bring you?